MY BOOK OF WOE...WHOA...

A Personal Journey of Triumph

By

Michelle Sommerset-Brown

Library of Congress Cataloging-in-Publication Data Sommerset-Brown, Michelle Lynette
1963 –

My Book of Woe….Whoa…….. A Personal Journey of Triumph
Created & Written by Michelle Lynette Sommerset-Brown

Printed in the United States
First Printing, 2017
IBSN 978-0-9985550-0-3
FIRST EDITION

My Book of Woe...Whoa...

A Personal Journey of Triumph

On September 27th, 2013, I had a rare surgery. My podiatrist broke my right ankle to replace an ankle joint (riddled with arthritis), with a cadaver joint. That was the beginning of one my most difficult "Walk-A-Bouts". I had no idea that this would be the least of four more horrible events that were to come; and ultimately ignite a metamorphosis in changing my original, Master-Life Plan. I started writing this book in March 2014. I planned on finishing it within a year. But horrific events kept happening to me, which hurled me into very unfamiliar territory. So writing became my escape, if you will; my case study of how to process the thoughts in my head, which I could not share even with my closest friends. This book, however, will not reveal my most coveted pain. I can't do it. It's still too painful.

Now it is April 2016, and I'm still writing. But on this day, April 4th I had an epiphany of sorts to help me stop this swirling, spiraling effect going on in my head. We will talk about that later.

This book was written for those warriors like me, who feel at the end of every day, all of your energy is completely spent. Am I getting too old for this, you ask yourself, because you know that you've been down this road before? The shadows are darker, the streets not as wide, and the roads are punctured with pot holes.

You are tired of fighting to make sure that everything is taken care of on a daily basis for your kids, your spouse, even your employer. Yes, you are always last in line for a handout, of sorts – and most of the time it is totally self-imposed. You walk around with a smile on your face at the appropriate time of course: greeting neighbors, or answering the phone when friends call. And you avoid conversing with them whenever you can. You know what it feels like – Your cheeks are propped up by some invisible force, your constant shadow companion. You are truly a walking zombie. But one with a smile plastered on your face. You have been doing this for so long, that it is now second nature; just like brushing your teeth every morning.

You do your best to glide through rehearsed movements and mannerisms reflected back at yourself, when you look in the mirror. After all, you have to maintain the veneer you've created for your life, until you find your footing again. There is a "dis-ease" about it all. It whispers the mantra that you will be okay; that this too will pass. But you're not so sure this time……….

"I feel lost and I honestly don't know what to do now." Can you imagine how devastating it is to feel lost at 50 years-old? This was supposed to be "My Year". I had everything planned. None of it, and I mean none of it came to fruition. But I'm still working on it.

I fooled myself into thinking that I was well on my way to reaching what at the time was my Master Life Plan. But events outside of my control have flung me in to a space that is not at all familiar to me.

My life decisions seem monumental. And as intelligent a woman as I am and have worked so hard to become, I literally do not know what to do at this phase of my life! It's hard to even admit that fact, but it's true.

I am compelled to write about how crazy everything seems to be in my world. Because of my faith, I have to trust that no matter what I see, and it's not pretty; hear, and it's always ugly these days, that God will propel me to the other side. Not just by the skin of my teeth, but triumphantly! How else can I keep my sanity?

This is a guide for the faint of heart, just like me. My hope is that if you find yourself on the edge and without a map, this book will be an effective guide back to a place of JOY and PEACE! I did not use the word happiness. Happiness is a momentary emotion. Joy and Peace can be experienced on a daily basis; yes, even in the midst of pain. It's all about the choices you make from the moment you wake up in the morning, until your last moment of consciousness each night. And don't forget that when worry taps you on the shoulder in the wee hours of the night, you still have the right to choose the path of your thoughts. What's the adage….as our thoughts go, so do our actions, dreams, desires, plans and lives.

Dedication

To my sons

David Kwan and Jarrod Benjamin

You guys taught me the true meaning of love, acceptance, laughter and most of all forgiveness

Even though life can be quite caustic sometimes, know this….

You Can Overcome Any Trial With God's Word In Your Heart And Your Buddy Jesus Christ ("JC") By Your Side

Try To Do A Better Job Than Mom Did. I Dare You!

I Dare You

Written by Hardwell

Performed By Matthew Koma

Forward

His Name Is Music

There is no way I could have written this book without weaving into the fabric of these pages my deep love of music and lyrics. Music and lyrics have transcribed my deepest thoughts and feelings, in a way which I have never been able to effectively articulate. The package of music and lyrics is the one <u>earthly thing</u>, which has taken me to heights and places in my mind like nothing else in this world has ever been able to do. In my mind, they are one. They have been my unseen friend and lover. They coddle me at night when I am weak and afraid. And they are one of the weapons for the current war that I find raging inside me. Most battles are, after all, in your mind. And for this reason, I have to share them with you…..Here's a sample of how I feel.

I initially wrote this entire book with lyrics of various songs which I thought were appropriate for each chapter. Then, after several months of research and frustration in determining the legal and financial steps necessary to add all of the songs I wanted to include, I decided to just note them for each chapter, and encourage you, the reader, to look up the corresponding lyrics; I am hopeful that you will create a playlist to listen to them as you read this book. You won't be sorry putting in a little extra effort in understanding what I was feeling, while navigating through some of the most challenging years of my life.

TABLE OF CONTENTS

CHAPTER ONE
The Faint of Heart

Theme From The Valley Of The Dolls

Written By Dorey and Andre G. Previn

Performed By Dionne Warwick

As this songs states, "When did I stop feeling sure, feeling safe, and start wondering why?" I keep hearing myself repeat one simple phrase, "What the hell is going on? I don't even know how I got here….and I sure don't know how to maneuver out of this overgrown, rain-forest. The machete in my hand is dull and useless." Nothing is familiar to me anymore. Not one damn thing. I feel like I'm treading water and holding my breath at the same time. Crazy right?

This book is for The Faint of Heart.

I am writing to you in the present-**tense**, because I am currently living through what I consider one of the most difficult periods in my life. I don't know what direction I'm headed in, or where I will end up. But I am moving, nonetheless. This, I know to be true. The other thing that I know to be true is this:

> ***God Is My Source for Everything.*** *Even when I feel like He is hiding from me, as I feel now.*

I'm scared. No, really afraid – for my future, which in turn directly affects my family's future – my husband and two sons. If I mess up, the whole thing collapses; as I am the primary bread winner, planner and strategist of the Brown Clan. I'm the "Go to Girl".

It used to be a title of honor for me. A banner I proudly wore. Now it's a title which I would gladly hand to another. Go on, take it.

I'm broken, without any known instructions for re-building. And I absolutely hate reading instructions. I wish I had some to read now, though. The one tool that I need now, for sure, is guerilla glue.

I often wish I had a life-crisis, guidebook; a ventilator per se, to help me breathe while I am struggling to survive simultaneous catastrophes. Yes, I have had thoughts that death might be an easier route out of these situations. I have to tell the truth of the full landscape of my momentary mindset. But my family needs me, and I refuse to leave them orphaned. Besides that, I am a Christian who loves the Lord. Hell is real; and I'm not trying to spend an eternity there. Menopause is hell enough for me, thank you.

I know God's will for me is not to give up. That does not mean that I feel hope in my heart now, although strangely it does exist in my mind. I am after all, human. Oftentimes, our feelings are not in line with what we carry in our thoughts. Feelings always follow your thoughts. Remember that life fact. They are stubborn and hardheaded like children, and must be parented, just the same.

I choose to stand, crutches in both hands, stabilizing the cadence of my rhythmic side-to-side movements. I'm not sure whether to step to the right, left, ahead or back. So I just sway. I can't say that I choose to fight any longer. There was a time when that would have been my canned reply – an automatic response. But I've found lately that life can have a rawness about it, which leaves one unable to devise a quick solution; a life detour, per se. So here I am, just standing, observing, praying, crying, watching and waiting, for a sign on what to do next.

I know what is at stake here: my faith, my home, my family, my sanity, and most importantly my walk with the Lord. I don't know what pieces to play in this real- life, chess game; at least not at the moment. Maybe by the time I finish writing this book, I'll have some snippet of revelation and wisdom to share. But no promises, okay.

Again, I'm it. If my house tumbles, we all fall. It's a heavy burden, when you are Fragile and you still have to be the Way Maker. Or so you perceive that to be the case.

Perception – That's such an interesting word. Let me think more about what that word really means to me. Maybe I will address it later on, as my journey unfolds. But for now, I've got nothing more to share on the subject.

I have made a decision. It is time to: Live My Life Out Loud.

"What does that mean," you ask? I have to write myself out of this state of dissatisfaction, by recording what I am feeling and facing. I must be truthful about it. However, there's one thing that happened to me, though, that I am not sure I will ever be able to share with you. That wound has a wicked scab on it. And I keep picking at it. Not sure if it will ever heal. We'll see. I hope to come out of this eclipse one day. The words for the pain I feel regarding this personal tragedy can't make it past my lips. It cuts way too deep. Never could I have imagined feeling such shock, pain and sadness.

I am in such a state of mind and physical stress that reading my bible does not help me as I write this chapter. I just shared this statement with a friend, and she was shocked. "No, not you Michelle", Maria said. Remember, I said I would be honest in my journaling. That is with what I can share……

I know that God is aware of my situation, but I don't know why He remains silent.

Silence - That's another word that I find so interesting. Let's tuck that word on the shelf as well. I can't promise that we'll find our way back to it. I can only say that it is a word that does not resonate within my Spirit the way it used to.

So, while literally holding my breath until the Lord speaks to me, my counselors are music, lyrics and journaling. Just as it is at the inception of any counseling session, no one knows what will come out of this exploratory journey. It's funny – I never considered myself a writer. I've fallen into it. It keeps my mind occupied, and out of the dark recesses of depression and despair.

There are several other reasons I am "Living My Life Out Loud" and journaling my personal story.

- I need to prove to myself that at the age of 50, my life is not over. I can do new things, better things, exciting things, which bring me peace, more security and financial independence than I have now. But these things will not bring me more love. My house is full of it. Yes and simultaneous anger and resentment. Love will always be here and possibly anger and resentment as well. But the latter two, I hope to learn to control by handing them over to God. That's the only recipe for true peace of mind.

- My hope is that this book will serve as a guide for others who are experiencing the same thing. I wish that I had one now.

- But most of all, I want my sons to have a survival guide to use, just in case I am not around to catch them.

CHAPTER TWO
Fragile

Wounds are the physical manifestation of a sharp blow.

Just as unseen cuts inflicted

on a fragile soul are wounds,

which are never forgotten.

Fragile, Written and Performed By Sting

It's so odd how one simple word, can completely sum up a moment in your life. I have been holding my breath for thirty-six months now. And although the pigment of my skin is a smooth, velvety, chocolate-brown, hues of black and blue are clearly noticeable. That is, if you are looking at me while wearing your spiritual glasses.

I have always been proud of the fact that I can "cloak" well. But even the best "cloaker" can't hide the color of despair. You know what cloaking is…. It's hiding in plain sight, like the Romulans did on Star Trek, The Next Generation. I loved that show, but hated the Romulans. I don't know why, because I like to hide in plain, sight just like them!

Perching on a moment of total collapse, my soul screams so loud that I know everyone had to hear me. But they dare not recognize my pain, lest it transfer its talons from me to them.

I don't know how things are going to end for me. But here's how everything started….

It was so easy. I landed a fabulous new job. Someone courted me to join a new financial services company, with a fresh vision for offering corporate banking services and expertise, within a community banking environment. My new role as a Treasury & Information Management Consultant and Senior Vice President for the State of Georgia and Northern Florida, not only involved my expertise as a seasoned sales consultant, but also the opportunity to work with a talented group of folks, to build the platform of our dreams, firsthand. Wow, you'd never get a chance to do this with a larger, more established Bank. I'd be crazy not to jump at the opportunity. And I considered myself totally sane at that juncture. The following year was uneventful. The job was not easy, but very satisfying.

Now I had been dealing with a bum ankle for over fifteen years. I had arthritis in my right ankle joint. I knew that surgery would help, but being a sales person, I needed to remain mobile to make money to support my family. But the pain was unbearable. It got to the point that any slight movement of my right leg across my bed at night, felt like someone froze my ankle and then popped it in half. My podiatrist ended up being a great life-coach for me. "Michelle – You can either stop to take care of yourself now, or wait until it's too late and let me put in a metal ankle replacement later. I can show you how to manage your boss and company, so that you can take care of yourself. You are too young for a metal ankle replacement; those parts only last ten years." "Dr. Harley", I said. "I need more time to make my yearly revenue goal. If you give me one more cortisone shot, I'll work harder on generating revenue and see you on the operating table in September."

I kept my word and so did he. But by September 27th, the day of surgery I still had not met my annual goal. I moved forward in faith anyway. The doctor had to break my ankle to put in a cadaver joint.

Then in December the unthinkable happened. The words to describe this life event will never cross my lips.

CHAPTER THREE
Walkabouts

We've all experienced our seasons of Walkabouts. When we hear this word walkabout, we automatically think of youthful, male Aborigines in Australia. For them, a walkabout is a rite of passage undertaken alone, in the wilderness, for a period that can last as long as six months. A rite of passage typically denotes a ritualistic event that promotes a person from one stage of development to a more advanced level, e.g. from adolescence to adulthood. Each member of society throughout history has participated in various forms of rites of passages. They are a normal and necessary part of human development. And oftentimes, we find ourselves graduating from these passages unaware of our actual participation in them.

One of my first rites of passages, which I was totally unaware of at the time, was when I learned to drive a car. It took a couple of years for me to perfect my skills, because you see, I started at the age of eight.

My sweet father was a driver's education teacher. He had a car that had a brake on the passenger side. If I was about to hit something, he stopped me with either his brake on the passenger side of the car, or his left hand on my side to change the direction of the steering wheel. That was awesome! I never had an accident thanks to dad. So when I got my driver's license at the age of 16, it was no big deal. I was just considered a legal driver in my mind. That rite of passage totally escaped me. To this day, I have fond memories of dad letting me, my sister and most of our neighborhood friends drive up and down Eleanor Street.

My dad has to have ancestral roots in Jamaica, because he had as many as four jobs at one time. He never slept, or I never saw him sleep much, that is. As an adult, my mom told me that he got fired from several jobs for falling asleep at night. They never told us that when we were young. I don't care anyway. My dad and mom are still my life heroes! Unfortunately as I started writing this book, my dad was 75 years old and suffering with Alzheimer's disease. He is led around primarily by my tired mother, totally unaware of his passage further into a wicked illness, and then into eternal bliss with the Lord.

One of my next rites of passage that I was again totally unaware of, at least in part, was my first job at an ice cream and sandwich shop. The ice cream and sandwhich shop was located on Savannah's famous River Street. It's still there, but the name and owners have come and gone with the wind. It was the summer of my junior year in high school, 1980. My mom's friend owned the restaurant. And let's just say, it was my first time meeting and working with gay men and working with folks who smoked the devil's lettuce, pretty regularly. I've already started laughing again. I was such a goof ball and so naive. This was one of the best times in my life and some of the best people that I have ever had the privilege of working with.

There were two gay guys who were cooks, and they could "throw down", as we say in the Deep South. They brought so much laughter into our work environment. I so looked forward to working with them each week.

Working in the store was like being in an African American barbershop. Even to this day, when I have the occasion (it's my husband's primary job), to visit our local and rather militant barber, I find that I hesitate to enter into any conversation. They are all smarter and for sure quicker mental processors than me. Don't get me wrong, I am a very intelligent individual with a BA in Accounting and an MBA. But I do not have the inherent urban street knowledge or quick wit to even think about participating in barbershop rhetoric. So to this day, I do now what I did back then: sit back, listen, laugh and learn what's really going on in the world. I can share one tip: "Don't believe what you hear on Fox News" – It's skewed like everything else, but more so than other media outlets. My seven year old son, Jarrod, reminded me of that fact one evening, while watching the Fox News channel. He said Mom, "Don't watch that channel. Mr. Reggie told us that they fabricate the truth". I just changed the channel. Mr. Reggie is way smarter than me.

One of the guys in the ice cream and sandwich shop, in particular, brought sadness in the store as well. Or should I say, "I noticed a shadow of despair follow him into our world one day." When I close my eyes, I can still see his face.

I went to work to open the store early as usual, and I saw Calvin standing on the edge of the drop-off to the Savannah River. No one stands on the edge, unless they are getting on a boat. It's way too dangerous. With one misstep, you'll find yourself in the Savannah River, which is known to have strong "under-tow currents". Meaning, "Watch out – this river will grab your toe and you'll never see the light of day again". Everybody in Savannah is aware of this fact. It happened to a neighbor of ours. But he purposefully jumped in. I think that he found himself in the same spot I am standing in now and just gave up.

When I saw Calvin standing on the edge that morning, my voice left me. I dared not call his name; I was afraid that I would startle him and make him fall in the water. And I did not want to go to a funeral that summer. I was way too happy for all of that nonsense. I absolutely hate funerals. And I will do anything to avoid them, even if family members talk about me. I sat there for thirty minutes, watching Calvin, trying to determine what would push him so close to the edge of life? I understand now.....

Here's another funny story about that summer. I remember the first time I saw everybody smoking pot in the restaurant cooler. I went home, such a priss, and told my mom, "How dare they expose me to such things." She laughed and said, "Just hold your breath when you go in there", and that's exactly what I did. If I had any clue what life would bring me, I would have inhaled too. I was such a prissy girl back then.

My main job at the store was to make sure that we were never out of any of our ice cream flavors. I had to actually pay attention to consumer buying habits, and anticipate inventory needs. I was so scared. That is so hilarious to me now. That was a huge responsibility to me at the age of 16. I often look back on that summer and laugh for so many reasons, except one. That's when I learned to make business decisions and to be comfortable with deductive reasoning; also known as educated guesses. What a fun time.

In essence, we've all been there. I've had lots of walkabouts; some were even fun. I actually got pretty good at maneuvering through most of them. But there's another type of passage, that if you have not gone through yet, you will.......

CHAPTER FOUR
Walk-A-"Bouts"

Everything's so out of control

Please take it all away

Blurry

Written By Jimmy Allen, Wesley Scantlin and Doug Ardito
Performed By Puddle of Mudd

Yes, it means exactly what you think. If you say the word out loud, it sounds horrendous. When I hear the word, I think of two phrases: "Go away" and "One of us will not be the victor".

Let's look at the actual meaning of the word, Bout: "A short period of intense activity of a special kind", as in occasional bouts of severe exhaustion. Now let's review several synonyms: attack, fit, spasm, paroxysm, convulsion, eruption, outburst, period, session, and spell.

Are you ready for me to stop?

I can remember with vivid detail, every Walk-A "Bout" I have experienced. They have all transitioned me from one phase of life, enlightenment, to a higher level. But I will tell you that if I had the power to skip each trial, I would have done it without ever looking back. If I could change God's mind, to take them away from me or shorten them, I would have done that too.

Walk-A-"Bouts" are guaranteed painful experiences.

And the duration can seem infinite! That's what makes them so scary. Walk-A "Bouts" have no favorites. They don't distinguish between the educated, blood lines, old or new money, the cool or the crazy. They don't respect Christians or non-Christians. And as a Christian, I always hoped that I would have an edge, per se, at least on the level of intensity and duration of my Walk-A "Bouts". Again, Walk-A "Bouts" have no favorites, and neither does God.

My heart and mind are in such a state of despair, and I'm a believer of the one True God. Or at least I thought that I was. I fight every day to maintain what I believe is true in life. Each of us has to determine our own "truths" for ourselves. I'm struggling more than ever, just to keep from losing my mind and all hope. If you ever lose HOPE, it's OVER.

Please be very careful of others who always try to impart their truths onto you. Liars always come in the form of "Truth Sayers". Just saying.....

CHAPTER FIVE
Broken

Broken Bridges Soundtrack

**Written By Kennedy, John Davis / Kidd, Tammi Lynn /
Lindsey, Christopher Marsh**

Performed By Lindsey Hun

I'm not young anymore. Ok, there – I admit it……..

I turned 50 on December 31st, 2014. At this moment when I am writing these words, I am still in the midst of recovering from two surgical procedures over the last nine months. One in September and the other in March. I have at least six more months of personal therapy to push myself through, to my new normal. Whatever the hell that may be.

My life is sooooo different now. Pain has become my uninvited suitor; the lover who won't let go. He's smothering me. I honestly can't remember what it used to be like not to feel him by my side.

As I mentioned earlier, my first surgery was on September 27th, 2013. Given that I was given a cadaver ankle joint, I was not allowed to walk for 3 months. It was terrible. I had to sleep on a twin bed downstairs in our family room. Our master bedroom is upstairs. During that three month period, I may have slept upstairs ten times.   I crawled on my knees to go upstairs and down stairs on my butt. Or my hubby just picked me up and carried me where I needed to go. I used one of those knee scooters to get around otherwise inside and outside of the house. My sixteen year old even had to let me get on his back, when my husband wasn't around, to get me to the scooter in the garage. All just to get my ass to the car.

The pain medicine was so harsh that I vomited constantly, and gained only two pounds during that recovery period. My hair was shedding and my personality even changed while on some of the harsher pain meds. I was in so much pain, that I felt compelled to try to take the medicine, even for brief moments of relief. I don't see to this day, how people get addicted to narcotics. The side effects are too horrific, for what seemed like momentary relief.

I started to learn to walk again that December. It was hard and took longer than I thought it would. People take for granted the smallest gifts, like remembering the cadence of walking. I forgot in just under three months, how to walk. Unbelievable.

Then it happened....December 7th came.

A tragedy so horrible, at least for me, that I dare not speak of it. I still can't openly talk about it. The words are caught in my throat and will be for an eternity. It's amazing how you can talk about almost anything, and then how some things affect you so deeply that you not only can't think of appropriate words to convey how you feel, but you also won't allow the words to pass your lips.

CHAPTER SIX
Revelation

December 7th

CHAPTER SEVEN
Shock, Disbelief, Anger

January

CHAPTER EIGHT
Resentment and Hatred

March – Surgery #2

CHAPTER NINE
Something Worse Happened

July 16th – God, where are You?

CHAPTER TEN
Can You Believe This

November Surgery #3

CHAPTER ELEVEN
Thoughts

I just can't seem to find a reason to believe that I can break free

Hold Me Jesus

Written and Performed By Big Daddy Weave

I think about life sometimes now as being a tangible and simultaneously intangible state of being. It's made up of varying elements, which are added to, detracted and even at times obliterated from our existence. A cocktail, if you can imagine it as such, where both good and evil exists in both the physical and spiritual realms. The ingredients are not always easily recognizable. They vary in potency depending upon one's environment, frame of mind and heart. These life elements have been mutating from the beginning of time, by the actions of man in the seen world, and the intuitive counteractions in the spiritual realm.

As I struggle to get my footing, I find myself desperately looking around my immediate space for someone with whom I can identify; one who, given a similar life experience, has successfully made it through to the other side.

"But I can't find you in the dark."

And even if I could find you, pertinent words that I would need to share for proper guidance can't find a path pass my lips.

All that comes to mind now are two words: Higher Faith.

There are those who lived before our time and those who live amongst us now, whom I believe have taken hold of the gift of Higher Faith. I call them the Enlightened Ones. These individuals, I believe, were given the same shot by God as all of us have been provided. I submit to you that possibly these Enlightened Ones took their shot, in whatever manner delivered to them, and peered in to the world as it truly exists (amongst the physical and unseen planes of existence). Did they make a conscious choice to follow the path of their spiritual ancestors? Will I make it through as well? I am fully convinced that my shot is upon me.

CHAPTER TWELVE
Enlightened Ones

Enlightened Ones have lived thousands and hundreds of years before us; even decades and days; and many walk beside us now. You are around them every day. You know them. If you don't, you're not paying attention to your surroundings. They aren't famous in man's eyes, but could easily be infamous in mine. Their hearts don't fret and run away on a daily basis as mine does now. They have the ability to stand on truths in a physical and spiritual sense; to successfully ride the storms of life, no matter how treacherous. But most of all, they are smiling in the midst of their pain.

They are the ones I want to talk to now. I need some of their wisdom. There are quiet truths and pain, which forge within us the belief that we can look up to our Source for relief. The question in my mind is "How much pain must I experience before crossing over?" I can say emphatically that I have had enough Lord. But my heart is still fretting. I'm still afraid. I still want to run away.

Run, Run, Run

Run with me

To a place with sweeping melody and reverie

Run with me

Run, Run, Run

Run with me

To a place where true acceptance lives

A place with no backlash or cynicism

A place where no one feels imprisoned, and shackled

No it hasn't made a sound. Has yet to come around, but still

Run with me

Run, Run, Run

Run with me

To where laughter lives

You know that we can be free, turning toward the laughing sun

Whewwwwww,

Run with me

Run

With me

By Michelle Sommerset-Brown

What more can I say. It's been this way since the beginning of time. It's embedded in each of us. Our souls long to burst forth the seeds that grow from within, and let us know that even if the stars fall from the sky, we are well.

People are chasing elusive highs. But I only have a need for peace now and the assurance that God is with me. As I am writing, I feel like I am not going to make it through all of the tragedies that have befallen me (physically and spiritually). Still I have HOPE. Not in my heart at this moment, but deep in my mind. My heart always follows what I hold true in my mind. I need it to catch up quickly, however.

The laws of men denounce the reality of what I need. Money can't help me. Neither can the counsel of friends. I can't even hear their encouraging words offered to me.

I **<u>choose</u>** to follow my mind and the promises of God, to walk in faith with the hope that I too will transition into an Enlightened One.

CHAPTER THIRTEEN

Is It Time To Change Your Master Life Plan ("MLP")?

Brand New Me

Written By Alicia Keys, Emile Sande, Neal Brian Conway, Crystal Waters

Performed By Alicia Keys

MLPs Are Never Static – How Flexible Are You?

What do you consider normal? I can't answer that question for you. So seriously, what do you consider normal in your life?

I am sure that you have thought out your life. How it will unfold, what your significant other will look and act like; even what funny tricks your future dog will do for you in the park on a Sunday afternoon. Make your plans, live your life. But be ready to make changes, because it's not going to unfold exactly as you have imagined. Why?

Because people are not perfect and life is tricky. Our lives can change drastically without an email alert.

Consider this…Everything for you as it stands now is fine, on cruise control. You're single, with a satisfactory social life and money left over after paying bills. What we old folks call disposable income. Or you are newly married and everything he/she does and says is so sweet.

You have time for fun, trips, plenty of friends. Your body is lean, smooth and tight. Maybe you have been with the love of your life for a while now, and are settling down to raise a family. You've got a good enough job to make ends meet. You actually enjoy your family and are on your way up the ladder socially and financially. You've achieved your Master Life Plan ("MLP"). Or so it seems.

Then a crisis hits……..Some event or series of events, outside of your control, which affect your viability as a mom, dad, husband, wife, lover, even as a friend. Your Master Life Plan is at risk. And you don't know how to maneuver in your new environment.

Are you still holding on to that same Master Life Plan that you developed eons ago? Suddenly you no longer recognize your life. The one you labored so hard to create. Your world is different now; why is your MLP the same?

As logical as I consider myself to be, it never occurred to me that it is perfectly fine and even necessary to tweak my MLP as situations in my life change. This one piece of vital wisdom hit me like a rock one day. There I was, attending a business conference to maintain my Certified Treasury Professional license, when the speaker did something rather refreshing. She talked about life and what really matters. She also said that it is perfectly fine to change your Master Life Plan, even if you reached it. What? At that moment, neither my age, my handicapped leg, my personal no-name crisis, nor the imploding company that I worked for, mattered as much to me as that vital piece of knowledge. The knowledge that I alone have the power to adjust my MLP at any point in my life cycle hit me over like a Mack truck!

I felt lighter on the trip back home. I knew that I had the freedom to make a major change. But did I have God's blessing? I had been toying around for at least ten years on writing a book. "But I'm no writer", I said to myself on many occasions. "I have an undergraduate degree in Accounting and an MBA, with a concentration in Finance." I thought that my MLP was in reach. But unforeseen forces rendered it ineffective. I looked for a new job in the same field for months now, while playing at writing. I talked to so many people; everyone told me I had a fabulous resume, but I could not get anyone to hire me. "What's going on God", I yelled one day. He did not answer me until I got really still one afternoon; that is until I was so tired and spent that I was receptive to hearing His voice!

God placed several scenes before me at this time. Mind you, this did not occur in one afternoon, but rather a period of about two months. There were many scenes of me driving the 60 miles to and from work each day. I had the biggest smile on my face each time I envisioned myself driving, albeit, in hectic Atlanta traffic.

And I was always listening to music.

God reminded me that these were often my most receptive moments to hear His voice. I had such inspirational thoughts and ideas around innovations during my daily commutes. I honestly forgot most of my inspirational thoughts since then. But not all of them. He showed me that I wasted the gifts/ideas He sent me so regularly. Maybe that's the price I paid for not receiving them. But I do remember two of them. One is writing. The other is so technical that I don't know where to start. I have to find a way to patent that idea before sharing further.

If you get to know my family, you'll quickly realize that baseball is a huge part of our lives. My kids have been playing since they were both about 7 years-old. And my husband has been coaching them for about that long also. I have spent so many hours on the baseball field, watching and cheering for my kids. Being happy for and simultaneously so jealous of my husband coaching them year-after-year-after year-after-year. He is someone who is ecstatic about the game. Baseball for my husband is what music and lyrics are to me. A slice of pure heaven. I'll tell you…at this moment as I write, I am listening to music. It catapults me to another dimension, where sadness, worry and fear have no invitation.

My husband was and still is always willing to stay up late, with little to no sleep (He works at night), just for the privilege to coach our sons. The truth is, I "hated him sometimes for coaching", because he adjusted his MLP to accommodate his love of coaching. It seemed above my need for him to go after jobs that fit in to my MLP.

But God showed me those scenes of him as well as those of me on the field, with my ear buds on – yep – listening to music, laughing and cheering for my boys, all while praising Him. You can't begin to know the number of innovative ideas revealed to me, sitting at a baseball park, surrounded by people, but only noticing one Spirit.

I am sooo high right now, that I imagine myself levitating on my knees at the pure magic of the marriage of music and lyrics. As I shared earlier, on that joyous day, when I take my first step in heaven I won't get pass falling on my knees in sheer joy. The heavenly music and lyrics will never cease, and I will simultaneously never get up from my knees in gratitude for spending an eternity on what I imagine will be the steps of Heaven. I apologize to you that I cannot better describe or provide a picture for you of what I feel and see during my magical and meditative states.

Let's get back on track. Where are you again in your MLP? How's it going? Is it time for you to make a change? Are you at a point in your life where you've bottomed out and your ground zero couldn't get any worse? Great – It's the perfect time to tweak your MLP.

CHAPTER FOURTEEN
Ground Zero

Breakout

Excerpt from Breakout

Written By Andy Connell, Corinne Drewery, Martin Jackson

Performed By Swing Out Sister

Life is bittersweet; full of happiness and despair. So when you find yourself at ground zero, any progress achieved from that point is so very precious. Being low causes you to look up to the one true Source (The Trinity – God, Jesus and the Holy Spirit) for peace, comfort and direction. You can't fall any farther, can you?

Look at things from this viewpoint: Failure can be refreshing. And in the aftermath of being battered by life, it opens your mind to the gift of cherishing each moment of success and simple joy that comes your way. As the saying goes, flowers only grow after being fertilized and watered!

There is honestly so much pain in my heart, that I have to believe I am living in what is likely to be, a period of exponential personal growth.

CHAPTER FIFTEEN
Sometimes You Have To Walk Alone

Alone Again (Naturally)

Written By Gilbert O'Sullivan, Nelson Candido Da Motta Filho

Let's face it. People are human. And because of this fact, you are going to either have to put on "Big Girl Panties" or "Big Boy Drawers", and walk through some trials, alone.

I'm not saying not to expect family and friends to help you get through trying moments. But I am saying don't be disappointed when no one is knocking on your door. And don't be angry about it. Simply enjoy those who show up (if they do at all), and forget about why others are not there for you. Some of my best friends have been there when I really, really needed them, and some of them were not around at all; and I really, really needed them. I still love all of them.

Realize that family members can be the worst at providing support. My sister never called me once throughout any of what you know at this juncture as my first three surgeries (I haven't mentioned the following two cancer surgeries yet, five in all), as did other family members. But I had girlfriends who were as close to me as I wish I were with my only sibling and some of my relatives. People that I thought would visit me, and lived just around the corner, down the street, even an hour away, never did. I was in such bad shape during those times. But there were equally people who barely knew me and showed up with meals for my family. I realized that I had to let go of anger and disappointment, and cherish those who stood by me, whenever they stood by me. My kids taught me to be grateful for those who showed they cared and forget anyone who did not.

Everyone Is Human, Just Like You.

CHAPTER SIXTEEN
Perception
No-One Goes Easily

Does your perceived truth give you the authority

to hurt others?

Do you feel that you have the right to do so?

Is your way the only way….

Belief

Written and Performed By John Clayton Mayer

I said that I'd find my way back to the word, Perception.

Two people can witness the same event, and their respective takeaways can be totally different, with both parties telling the truth – as they experienced it.

This is such an interesting topic for me. A person's perception is his/her respective reality, even if they experience a simultaneous event with another individual. Perception can cause strife, anger, hatred and even death. It feeds, for better or for worse, a person's belief system.

Sometimes we think that we are so spot on about something. And in actuality, arc not even playing on the same baseball field with our teammates. True self-actualization occurs when you can be honest with yourself, and open up to the possibility that the role you are playing or have played in a given situation may not be genuine. It requires you to process, objectively, events outside of the arena of self. You must be an Enlightened One to practice the art of true self-actualization. Because only Enlightened Ones can open their eyes and minds to see and understand that they are not always the victim.

Your ability to be self-aware could in fact dissuade caustic thoughts and actions towards others. If you relax and allow yourself to view your actions and thoughts objectively, you may see, firsthand, that your life in general will be a more peaceful one. And by chance you will help others to have a more peaceful existence, in your presence, as well.

It's prudent to evaluate your perception of events and the possibility of how others could have a different viewpoint. It may provide you with the gift of accepting people who are in a different lane than you on the highway of life. You don't have to live in the lane that another chooses to drive in, but it sure would help you see the road more clearly, if you could acknowledge that there are, in fact, multiple lanes on the highway of life which are headed to the same destination.

CHAPTER SEVENTEEN

What To Do When You Haven't Got A Clue

Be Still and Keep Moving Forward

Hold On

Written By Moses Peter Pelham, Martin
Performed By Fred Hammond, James Fortune, FIYA, Monica

You can relate, right! I'm sure. There will be times when you may have to dummy down on life to get a grip on what's facing you, head-on. Meaning, you have to keep moving, but stay still at the same time. I know, I know. You're thinking, "Michelle – What are you talking about? That's an oxymoron if I ever heard one. Keep moving but stay still too?"

Yes that's exactly what I'm saying. You can do it. I've lived it, and it may save your sanity one day! It's true. Life gives you curves and if you are to survive, you have to learn to swerve.

It's September now, and my dad is dying. My Walk-A-"Bout" just took a forty-five degree turn!

Dad is in the last stages of dealing with Alzheimer's disease. My mom is in the last stages of desperately trying to hold on to him. She is clearly in early stages of dementia; denial-dementia is more like it. And my sister is clearly in the early stages of pure an unequivocal rage.

I took the picture above of my then 15-year old son and my dad on the streets of downtown Savannah. This picture is very symbolic of my dad's passing in to another realm of eternity. I didn't realize it when I took the picture, but now I see it as my son and dad saying goodbye to each other. You see how they are standing at the very edge of the shadow, which to me represents the world we all live in now. Dad is getting ready to cross over to Paradise. They both have their heads bowed, because they know that they will be separated for a while. God gave me the gift of taking this picture at this exact moment. And it took a year for me to see the significance of the light, the shadows, the bowed heads and a grandson holding a grandfather's hand, just before the grandfather steps into eternity! Paradise is bright, warm and inviting. Look at the bright light in the upper left of the picture. And if you look to the right it looks like there is a small rainbow to walk under. This picture always makes me cry, because God gave it to me as a gift and a promise!

On the same day that I got the call that dad stopped eating and drinking, I had a doctor's appointment with my podiatrist. I kept repeating to myself, no more surgeries, no more surgeries. I was fully aware walking in to the doctor's office that the level of pain I was still living with was totally unacceptable. Sure enough, I called my husband after the visit to share that I had to have yet another surgery; this time to cut my achilles tendon. Remember that I had been in pain every day since my first surgery on September 27, 2013. I asked the doctor if this was my new normal, and he said absolutely not. It didn't help that I was 50, with diabetes. That's another secret that I tried to hide for so many years. After viewing the MRI, it was determined that this too would be another major surgery. Damn! Broken was exactly how I felt that day.

I live four hours away from my parents. My family relied on help with my dad from multiple sources: family, friends, hospice and long-term healthcare workers. Gees – It really does take a village to take care of kids and aging parents.

On any given day, I found myself talking to as many as five different people about the current state of both of my parents. Last week mom scraped the side of her Porsche on the garage and got lost going to the doctor. She denied both events of course. The car dent is readily apparent. She looked surprised when I showed her and wondered who was driving her car. She's in such a state of denial. It's a coping mechanism. But it is truly driving me crazy.

I started writing this chapter on September 6th, 2014. Dad died on October 1st. I returned home on October 10th, and today, October 21st is my first day back to attempt to complete this Book of Woe. So much has happened since then.

I'm not sure where to start, so I'll just jump in with a quick summary. My sister hates me and is very angry because my parents appointed me Power of Attorney and made a will without her orchestrating or authorizing the details of its content. She is a very hateful person and you can never achieve anything with two chiefs leading a tribe; especially if one walks down the path of peace, and the other sheer chaos. One seeks to encourage and build up, and the other takes every opportunity to tear apart and annihilate, whenever possible just for kicks. This is, my perception of what initiated my sister's rage and consequential unethical acts of tricking my mother to sign over to her Power of Attorney status and change the will to what she considered as "now a fair will". She got my mother to sign over Power of Attorney after being fully documented by a physician as having dementia and needing to be placed in a secure and locked environment providing assistance with daily activities.

My mom said very ugly things to me after my dad died. She denies saying them, and I'm not truly convinced that she forgot everything she said, as she claimed. She has always been a rather mean-spirited individual, just like my sister; and boy I'm catching it from her now because she is angry that my dad left her. He's the lucky one!

My aunt went off on me and my mom when we shared with her that we were not planning on having a wake, because we were exhausted and did not feel as though we could survive a wake the night before the funeral. To dispel the drama and disrespect vomited towards my mom and me, in five minutes, I put her on hold and arranged and paid for the wake out of my own money. I had to quickly dispel the drama thrown my way. I don't handle drama well, and certainly not when coupled with grief. Then I apologized to my mom and told her that she did not have to come, but I needed to save my sanity by reducing all of the drama that I am not accustomed to. My cousin called me the day before and warned me about my Aunt's reputation at family funerals. I did not remember that part of her, because I left home at the age of 17, and really only talked to her on the phone no more than four or five occasions since I left home. Remember that at this point, I am now 50 years-old. My cousin shared with me that my aunt interrupts family funeral programs, says whatever she feels like saying, and then breaks in to song. And "GOT DAMNIT" (that's the only way I can say that phrase); she did that very thing, down to the same song. It's funny now, but I was so livid when it happened. All I could do at that point was to literally shut down and not acknowledge her presence. I was surprised that it was so easy for me to do not to acknowledge her presence. It was an innate coping mechanism that I was a virgin to, but when needed it easily kicked in for me. At that moment, she no longer existed to me, as if an invisible veil was placed over my head; one that would not allow me to let her in my personal space or touch me. Those two acts, of silence, represented un-forgiveness to me. And to violate those two very distinct acts, would mean the ultimate disregard for my sense of self. In a strange way, it was like I was given a directive to stay the course and stand against her mistreatment in silence. That's how I made it through such a devastating week for me. I didn't get to mourn until the next week when I returned home. I didn't have time. And when I returned to my parent's home each night, I would try to get to my room as quickly as possible, to attempt to avoid my mother's wrath at my father's passing. She followed me every night.

So I found myself in yet another unfamiliar place.

As I shared earlier, my sister did not help at all with any arrangements. She and mom had words two weeks before dad died and she never called Mom to see how he was doing. She flew in the night before and out the day of the funeral. I totally understood, but it was so hurtful to be on the receiving end. I planned the funeral and wake pretty much by myself, and stayed afterwards to get dad's benefits transferred over to Mom.

Mind you, I am no angel. My flesh got in front of me as well during some very trying moments.

But my eyes were opened to another level of God's Sufficient/Daily Grace.

For roughly ten days I promised myself that I would consume at a minimum, for nourishment's sake, a piece of fruit and bottle of water. I never promised myself that I would eat or drink anything for the rest of the day, however. I slept on average no more than three hours a night. Rightfully so, every day people honked their horns at me for making bad driving decisions. I had to have individuals repeat what they said to me multiple times to get my brain to process what they were trying to convey to me. I was utterly exhausted.

During that week, I could no longer say that mom had severe memory challenges. In less than ten days, we were the same: tired, exhausted, empty and grief stricken. I realized that given my mom lived in this world for three years taking care of dad, that her memory might not be as challenged as I originally thought. I am still learning to let go, and allow her to have the independence she wants and demands; but it's difficult because she is not altogether well. Of course, I am always watching from afar. I just no longer see the need to micro manage her life. Clarity is a great gift for everyone.

On a daily basis I was physically, mentally and spiritually depleted. Each night I asked got to lift my burden, and He did not. I told God every night that I did not know what to do and desperately needed to hear from Him. I heard nothing. But every morning I got up, still wounded from the previous days' scars, able to miraculously hug and kiss my mean-spirited mom to start at it all over again. That was God's Grace; only a daily portion for me. Every night I found myself again with a gauge set at EMPTY!

So when you find yourself in the valley and the dirt starts to give way, keep moving but stand still. Keep moving in the worldly sense of accomplishing whatever daily tasks are before you. You won't remember the majority of the tasks achieved in a given day. Still you have to move forward. But be still in your heart and mind. Observe what is happening to you and around you. And wait on God. He may reply with a word from multiple sources. He may be quiet, for a time and it's possible for even an eternity. But remember that He is always with you. He promises to provide Grace sufficient for the day. It says it in His word, and I can truly say that God's promises are true!

Oh He is the One

Yes, it is God's Son

Who holds your Hand?

As tiny as a grain of Sand

Deliverance Provided

When your world has Collided

On the edge of Joy and Death, it Seems

Not sure whether this is a Dream

Your Life Transcended in the space of one's Breath.

Oh, He Is The One

By Michelle Sommerset-Brown

CHAPTER EIGHTEEN
Blows
That's Not The Way It Feels

They say blows fade with time

I've learned to live with them

But that's not the way it feels

Operator

Written and Performed By James J. Croce

How much invisible baggage are you walking around with every day? Be honest.

Has anything affected you so deeply in your heart and mind that it softly influences the decisions you are making today, or better yet how you respond to someone if they trip across one of your hidden triggers?

Don't kid yourself. You are shaped by your surroundings in some major or minor way. Blows are just like they sound. Did someone break your heart; someone you really, really trusted? Did someone betray you, or villainize you without cause? Heartbreakers aren't always of the opposite sex. Maybe someone said that your voice sounds funny; "Do you really speak like that?" Yep, it happened to me. And being such a shy person in college, I was so humiliated. Especially because it was a cool frat guy that made fun of me in the middle of the University of Georgia student commons area. Did a boss ever tell you that you did something so well, but then chimed in with a negative comment he really wanted to bring home to you? Has someone close to you said that they don't like you, or want to be around you and you can't figure out why? Maybe he/she is your sibling and you want to be close, but they keep pushing you away?

Blows. They hurt.

Does time really heal all wounds? Not always. There will be some pains in your life that will diminish, but never go away. It's okay though. The important thing I believe is to recognize why you behave and react to certain people and situations. Sometimes our history plays far too great a part in our current life responses. Just be aware of yourself, your past and how certain events cast a shadow on your present life.

Never lie to yourself. You don't have to prove to anyone, including your-self, that you've overcome a blow. No matter how long ago the pain started.

You will be able to move on, blows and all. You can still have a happy life no matter what has happened to you.

Consider this; your pain could be your greatest blessing. Healing may come through your tears. Pain causes you to seek something or some-one other than yourself for relief. And there He is, standing in the wings, waiting for you to turn your face His way. The pain I felt the week of my dad's death helped me to know that I know that I know that God still lives and is my constant Helper. My greatest disappointments have proven to be such blessings. As I revisit this chapter I am 52 years old waiting to turn 53 on the 31st. It's December 7th again (oh my good-ness) and my heart is heavy. I don't know where my mom is….my sister moved her without telling me.

But even though another trial has beset me, I can still say to you…"Hap-piness is a choice." Protect your right to choose happiness daily. Focus on what you mentally know is true, and allow your heart to catch up. Emotions should always play second fiddle to what you know is true, e.g. God's promises in His Book of Love to us (Bible). God will always cause you to be triumphant in the end. Wait on Him!

Always know that it's important to face your pain, even when it surpris-ingly resurfaces over the most trivial of events. You know yourself better than anyone, just recognize what's going on and talk yourself through it; in a loving manner; just as you would talk to your spouse son, daughter or best friend.

49

CHAPTER NINETEEN
The Art of Silence

Declaration (This Is It)

Written By Kirk Franklin, Kenny Loggins, Michael MacDonald

Performed By Kirk Franklin

There is power in Silence.

Yes, it's true. Silence can oftentimes wield more power in effecting change in the heart of man, than the most eloquent speech. I've witnessed the effects of it in my own life, just today. I am writing this Chapter as a result of a phone call that I received this morning, January 2, 2015.

Remember the aunt I spoke about earlier? The one who was so ugly to me during my dad's funeral? Remember my two directives, executed in silence: not letting her infringe upon my personal space and not allowing her to touch me? These two behaviors where the only solutions I came up with to cope with experiencing a dramatic life event, which I had to walk through under public scrutiny. My aunt's public act of disrespect at dad's wake was juicy gossip and continued gossip for those individuals showing up the next day at the funeral. I was determined not to make a scene. That kind of behavior is not in my make-up. Sometimes I wished that it were, though.

Silence allowed me to execute on those two directives without displaying the ugliness that was so easily shown to me and my mother. It was hard,

but I knew that it was the correct path to take on so many levels.
I needed to:

- Respect my sense of self

- Respect my family's name

- Be a parent who led by example in not to matching the ugly behavior shown towards me and my mom; even though I had the right to do so.

She called this morning to apologize and ask my forgiveness. Of course I would give it to her, and am most appreciative for her reaching out to me. See, silence does work. If you let go and as they say, "Let God" handle things, His actions will leave you speechless! But I won't forget. Always remember that people will always show you who they truly are inside.

Forgive, but don't forget. Potential is just that; waiting in the wing for another appearance!

CHAPTER TWENTY
The Art of Visualization

Today is my 51ˢᵗ Birthday. It's the last day of the year, and boy, I am so happy to say good riddance to 2014!

We've all heard and believe to a certain extent that we become what we focus on. Yes, visualization or the ability to consistently view your desires/dreams, within the context of being able to see who you want to become, where you want to be and whom you want to be surrounded by, is a skill that everyone on this planet needs to sharpen. I'll even go as far as saying that there ought to be a class taught in elementary school and thereafter through post-graduate studies on this topic.

I received a tasty chocolate cake from a friend visiting me on my birthday. My husband lit it for me and presented it to me. As I was blowing out the candles, I found myself blowing away all of the horrible events I experienced over the past year. It only took seconds, really. But in those few moments I had experienced a release of sorts and had a revelation!

I knew at that moment, I had to remember all of the details of blowing away or literally letting go of my fears, doubts, bad experiences, etc. I knew that I needed to remember, <u>for the rest of my life</u>, what blowing out that candle looked like to me; what it felt like to allow my breath to escape my body and relax; what two phrases (it's okay, you are protected) came to mind as I released my darkest moments out into the universe, in one smooth and very quick breath.

I did not have the intelligence to know that this moment would be a critical meditative exercise for my future self. It was a simple gift, which I had the good conscience to embrace at a moment's notice.

You too will be given, "simple gifts" from God. Open yourself up to be receptive and aware of the tiniest lessons offered from above. They may one-day save your sanity and ability to cope within the recess of dark-life moments.

CHAPTER TWENTY-ONE

Release Your Pain Through Forgiveness

The art of forgiveness is only perfected through pain

Jesus, Friend of Sinners

Written By Matthew Joseph West and Mark Hall

Performed By Casting Crows

In order to have an original life, you are going to have to learn to forgive.

I didn't say forget.

I don't believe that our human condition allows us to truly forget pain inflicted upon us by others. The ability not to forget actually can work in our favor at times, by providing us with an early, inward alarm system.

Shame on you, if you keep making the same senseless mistakes, over and over and over again. I have been ashamed of myself on several occasions for doing this very thing. But I've learned from my mistakes.

Don't let past hurts and traumatic events prevent you from living a fruitful and happy life. Forgive others; forgive yourself too. Be brave in daily living and pursuing your dreams, but by all means don't be stupid!

I'll share with you a forgiveness exercise that I taught myself. When your memory brings up hurtful actions imposed on you by others, STOP. Take note of the thoughts going through your mind. Are they thoughts of anger, hatred, or loathing? It's important to be aware of what you are thinking and feeling, so that you can take it to the cross. At this point, I encourage you to genuinely pray for those who are causing your mental pain. This is an act of selflessness, but it is a powerful exercise; one that is the impetus for true forgiveness.

If you can learn to capture your negative thoughts about others and take them to the cross, JC (Jesus Christ) will be happy to take it from there. This is what I call conscious forgiveness.

It took me a long time to forgive others and myself for allowing others to cause pain in my life. But as I practiced conscious forgiveness, it made more room in my heart to concentrate on furthering my life on a several fronts: spiritual, mental and physical levels.

When you lack the ability to forgive others, it only hurts you.

Many of those individual's whom I spent numerous hours hating for their hurtful actions toward me, never had a clue what they did to me and how it affected me. But I learned that I too played an active role in the pain I allowed in to my life as a result of the actions of others. Only if you value the opinion of an individual, will they be able to cause you pain. Stop wasting your limited resource (TIME) on people who don't deserve it.

 Life has no remote. Get up and change it the old fashioned way!

CHAPTER TWENTY-TWO
Life Fundamentals

Last weekend I was at my youngest son's all-day baseball tournament. At the beginning of the game, our team was in the lead. The other team players made so many field errors that it looked like the game was ours to lose. Then one of the parents from the other team yelled out to its players, "Okay guys, you need to execute baseball fundamentals".

You will hear coaches/parents yell this phrase if their team is making a lot of fielding errors, and doing a pretty good job of giving the game away to the opposing team. Sure enough, the opposing players started executing their baseball fundamentals and whipped our butts – badly!

There are baseball fundamental plays for every position on the field. I won't bore you with reciting all of them, but I will share with you some of the well-known catch phrases:

- Set Your Feet

- Follow Through With Your Bat

- Keep Your Eye On The Ball

- You've Got A Full Count On You (2 strikes and three balls)– Now Protect Home Plate

After seeing the results of that game, I started wondering if there were Life Fundamentals that I could use, to help bridge me through the challenging circumstances I felt were crushing my spirit. I looked at the same list I shared with you above, and realized that I could transfer those exact rules to my personal circumstances. What a revelation.

- Set Your Feet (Don't Let A Perceived Disaster Move You. Breath. Ask for God's Guidance. Listen to The Instruction He Provides)

- Follow Through With Your Bat (Seek Godly Guidance and Follow His Instructions. Move Forward in Faith)

- Keep Your Eye On The Ball (Keep Your Eye on Jesus – No Matter What, Move Forward in Faith)

- You've Got A Full Count On You (2 strikes and three balls)– Now Protect Home Plate (Feed Your Spiritual Person – Daily. Don't Allow Satan To Steal It From You. Move Forward In Faith)

Life, just as in baseball, is all about mechanics. The mechanics of how you approach life through the good times, but most importantly the really, really tough times. If you dummy down, laying down all of the unnecessary noise around you and go back to Life Fundamentals, you will see a breakthrough. This can call for various mechanics, depending upon your position on the field of the game of life. But first, you have to figure out what position you are playing.

For me, at this moment, I have to focus on faith not fear, getting rest, learning how to stand my ground and when to simply talk or shut up. See I always know when to be quiet; I'm just not good at executing that particular fundamental play. Yes, my life would be so much easier if I could just keep my mouth shut more often. It's true. I have had the bad habit of feeling like I need to prove myself to people, even to those who don't deserve one ounce of my energy or attention. That's one of my unconscious MLP activities that I am working very hard on changing. Another one is resting in the strength of silence and allowing God to fight my perceived battles. Or better yet, allowing God to show me what I am doing wrong in a particular setting. Again, there is so very much strength in just being silent and resting in the fact that you are not required to have an opinion on everything.

Silence is strength, not a weakness as I used to believe. But it takes wisdom to recognize that fact. How wise are you?

59

CHAPTER TWENTY-THREE
Let It Go

Don't You Worry "Bout A Thing"

Written and Performed By Stevie Wonder

Just let it go, already.

You're grappling to keep your sanity, your family intact, your semblance of control, and what you feel life should be in the world at this particular time. Take a leap of faith into what may be the unknown for you; a life with Jesus by your side. Embrace the fact that you have no clue, no magic guerilla glue to paste your life back together. Do you even want the same life anyway?

Does it resonate anywhere in your spirit that the road you have chosen has reached a dead end? No cul-de-sac in sight where you can at least turn around. But a dead end on a dirt road with ditches on both sides. You are stuck. If you just let go of the tight hold you have on an existence that for all intents and purposes is crumbling in front of you, your arms will be wide open to receive a better life. One designed for a higher purpose. We each live in a fallen world where adversity is a given, not an option.

You can be an Enlightened One. But the path starts by accepting Jesus as your personal Savior.

Some things require believing. You're close enough to a breakthrough. Even though you know that your current intake of breath could be your last; it's still not too late to turn the table. You don't have to walk alone. But you do have to make a choice on who your spiritual companion will be on your life's journey.

Do this…

Imagine that you and the Lord are sitting alone in a bare room at a table for two. On your side there's nothing. Absolutely nothing. No napkin, no fork, no plate, no water to drink, nothing. You know that Jesus is on the other side of the table, but a partition blocks your view.

You are hungry and thirsty. Your hands have grasped the corners of the table at both ends so tightly that they have started to bleed. You are in the midst of a Walk-A-"Bout"! You can smell a feast, bountiful and nourishing. It is on Jesus' side of the table.

You think that you can turn the table to enjoy His feast on the other side by physically grabbing the table and forcing it to turn. It won't budge.

You can hear his voice speaking to you in a whisper; it is so soft and tender, shrouded in gentleness and peace. That's not what you are feeling, and you are both seated at the same table. Your side of the table is barren and God's side is plentiful. The aroma of His feast has penetrated your core; so much so that your mouth is watering. Your hands are bleeding more, because your grasp has tightened. You are so hungry and thirsty, so very thirsty. But you can't figure out why you are suffering with Christ so close to you? Out of despair and pure fatigue, you let go of your grasp.

All of a sudden you realize that the feast that God has waiting for you is still as fresh and warm as when it was first prepared. All you had to do was to just " Let Go".

When you find yourself in the midst of a "Walk-A-Bout":

Don't Panic➜Ask for God's Guidance➜ Follow His Instructions (Bible)➜ Move Forward In Faith

You're change is going to come. Sometimes pure exhaustion and fatigue is the only way God can get us to let go. He's waiting for you. But you have to make a cognizant choice. Of course He will set the stage to guide you down the road that does not have a dead-end or ditches on both sides, but it may have trials along the way. There's a new direction ahead for you; a route to peacefulness and eternity. But you have to make the choice to release your grip. A path chosen with God's guidance is never a dead-end path.

The plans that life in this world make, will put an end to you. You better learn to Let Go and Let God.

From now on it will be easy, so easy for you and me. It's been a life-long struggle. Just Let Go.

It's okay.

Cry if you need to.

But know that if you let go, and look up instead of around you, the joy of the Lord will encompass you. You can't play it safe anymore.

You have to lean in, kneel in, and press in to the Mighty Right Hand of God. You don't need a master's degree. You don't need a PhD. The less education you have, the easier it will be to let go.

You can't control anything anyway. So stop trying. And by all means don't try to bribe God. He will always present you with the ultimate option, intended for your good and not your harm. You just have to let go and lean in…… to Him.

It's all so crazy now. Take a look at yourself, carrying on outside of your ability to effect change. You have no power, but you also have all the power necessary to choose a more joyful path in life. Not through your own hands, but by the will, and sheer Grace of God.

Wake Up, And Let Go.

CHAPTER TWENTY-FOUR
Seek Inspiration in Daily Affairs

I Can't Go For That (No Can Do)

**Written By Melissa A. Elliot, Daryl Hall, Sara Allen,
John William Oates,
Brycyn Jamari Malykke Evans, Roosevelt III Harrell**

Performed By Daryl Hall and John William Oates

Yes, there are bright spots in the depths of despair. But you have to open your mind to that possibility. I'm in no way speaking of major parting of the skies, just bright spots. Whispers of joy and happiness that we each can take advantage of in our daily lives. Laughter is the easiest blessing to recognize. Have you ever felt a cool breeze on a hot day, heard an old, favorite song on the radio that wouldn't allow you to be sad, even if for only 3 minutes? While I'm writing this chapter and yes listening to music, I'm laughing while listening to Hall & Oates "I can't go for that". I even paused in my writing to enjoy the moment. Now that's what I'm talking about. I love the horns in that song. Pausing again, to dance …

I'll be back.

See what I mean? It's simple… Seek inspiration, joy, laughter, blessings in daily affairs. If you open your mind, these blessings will hunt you down. Try it! You are worth it, aren't you?

Dig deep inside of yourself. Life is made of millions of moments. But you must purposefully practice finding daily joy in the small things, until the bigger blessings come along. It's a great tool for managing the stress of daily living and loving.

CHAPTER TWENTY-FIVE

Forward, Forward, Forward…
And…Stop

He Knows My Name

Written By Francesca Battistelli, Seth Mosley, Mia Fieldes

Performed By Francesca Batistelli

I didn't know it at the time, but a 17 year old as they say, "Dropped Some Knowledge" on me during my family's white water rafting trip one summer, in Bryson City, N.C.

It was August 1, 2014. Our rafting trip lasted for roughly two and a half hours. That day started out with the warm summer sun, beckoning through the tree laden banks of the river. But halfway through the trip, we were met with rain. The funny thing about that day was that the cold rain was ten times warmer than that frigid river water which originated in the mountains of North Carolina.   We were barraged with frigid, churning ice-water! When we go back next summer, I am sure to rent one of the wet suits.

Joseph (Joe) Gleiter, our guide, taught me a new Life Fundamental that day which resonated with me and will stay with me for the remainder of my days.

You know, repetition is one of the best ways to learn. As I shared earlier, our rafting trip took over two hours to complete. And what Joe said over and over again changed my life, profoundly.

I want you to Know a few things about me, and Notice a few things on the pictures below.

Know This

- I am not a water person, at all.

- I can swim a little. Can't tread water at all. My husband and kids are excellent swimmers.

- I am actually uncomfortable in water, but very comfortable looking at it…. from the shore.

- I am afraid of deep water, and fish all around me. Yes, it's funny but true.

So when I told my family that I made reservations to go white water rafting in the mountains of North Carolina, everyone laughed at me. This was an attempt to face one of my fears head on.

Let me take you to the beginning.

Last summer I had to attend a business meeting at the Biltmore Estates in Asheville, N.C. My husband and one son traveled with me. We drove up through the back roads of North Georgia, and unfortunately missed our turn on the last leg of the trip. But fortunately for me, we found ourselves driving up the mountains of Bryson City, N.C. It was a beautiful summer day. The sun was bright. It wasn't hot at all. The winding road was lined with trees, everywhere. So we rolled down the windows and suddenly came upon a very long trail of white water rafters. Getting lost in the mountains that afternoon was another God given gift. I had great fun that day. The landscape and sounds in my head are still so vivid. The soft breeze-coddled tree branches looked like a lover in heat. I heard laughter at different levels – kids, adults, single and communal laughter; the river went on for miles. Then I saw it…someone was standing in the middle of the river, with the water only up to his waist. I said to myself, "I can do this. I will be back next year". That's how it all began.

Remember – Seek Inspiration In Daily Affairs.

So, I kept my promise to myself, and close to a year later, there I was on a two and a half hour fantasy rafting trip with the Brown Clan; in the coldest water, EVER!

Notice This

You see happiness and joy on my face. Throughout the entire trip, I was never afraid and that was totally due to my guide, Joe. You see the churning water don't you, and the simultaneous laughter on my face. From the beginning to the end of the trip, any time we approached a rapid, Joe would say," Forward, Forward, Forward……And….Stop."

There were times when Joe said forward, and I consciously peddled backwards, while thinking, "Really, I know you see how rough that water is ahead Joe?

But he never corrected me; he never once said, "Michelle, what are you doing? That's wrong?" He only adjusted his steering to compensate for any errors we made. He was calm the entire time. And no one fell out of our raft during the entire trip. He gave us instructions on how to secure our feet in the lip of the raft, to prevent us from falling in the icy water. At the beginning of the trip, they warned everyone to steer clear of "Jaws", a huge rock in our path that could cause serious problems. At the first turn, a kayaker hit Jaws head on, and both her paddle and kayak preceded her down the river, albeit in separate directions. We weren't even on the raft more than five minutes, before the first boater fell out. Joe was in such control. Steering to catch that kayaker's, wayward paddle, was a walk in the park for him. We couldn't catch the kayak, though, thank goodness! I gladly watched it pass us by. I didn't get cocky though. We had a long way to go!

That water was so, so, so, so very cold. Whenever we entered calm waters, we had to take our foot out of the raft's lip, because the cold water made it painful for our feet. But when we approached another rapid, automatic, feet in and Joe's guiding mantra, "Forward, Forward, Forward….And…..Stop".

Life is just like those rapid waters we experienced that day. Sometimes it's smooth and sometimes it's churning. You can go under it, be enveloped by it, exposed to it and even knocked out by it. It can be chilly and at times too cold for human exposure. It can also cause pain when it's too cold, where you feel like you have to step back, take your foot out of the lip, per se, and reset for the next churning event.

But you still have to move "Forward, Forward, Forward……And…. Stop".

You can come out victorious. Let Jesus be your guide. He can adjust your path safely, even if you are paddling in the wrong direction.

You just have to Trust Him like I trusted Joe that day.

CHAPTER TWENTY-SIX
I Know You

Even if the sun refuses to shine, even if I lose my mind, I know this to be true….. I know who You are……. You walk with me…….Every day.

Overcomer

Written By Benjamin Glover, Christopher E. Stevens, David Arthur

Performed By Mandisa

Why when faced with what you perceive as mounting obstacles, is your outlook shaded gray? Why even after you have successfully walked through past obstacles, is your view still tainted, daily?

Let's dive a little deeper here: Why as a Christian, after you and Jesus have successfully walked through countless storms, are you still afraid, still wanting to run away, still crying out that He has forgotten you? You in fact know the truth, but you allow your emotions and miss-perception of the surmounting obstacles before you to jade your ability to see yourself as an Overcomer.

Each day God offers us Grace….the ability to embrace JOY- Not Fear. Fear can grip hold of you tighter than a lover ever could; it is what you have to consciously recognize is at play in your life, and take thoughtful steps to counter its hold on you.   Faith is not inherent. It's a trained habit, which Enlightened Ones accomplish with ease!

You know how it feels when something gets in your eye. It hurts so badly. You open your eye to look for it. You feel the pain, but see no evidence of the culprit. I have often walked around with pain in my eye for several minutes, hours and even days, before finding the tiny piece of dirt which caused so much discomfort. Even after having other people peer into my eyes, sometimes I have not been able to find that damn little irritant. It dilutes everything else that I am doing, both physically and mentally, because it's there and won't let me forget that it is controlling me, in a sense. And yes, small irritants have often colored my outlook on whatever else I was trying to focus on at the time.

Today you may find yourself back in a familiar place, saying here I go again. But, just as He has in the past, this time too, God will offer you Grace sufficient for today's trials. The trick here is that He offers you Grace. It's up to you to embrace the gift. Think of it as an opportunity for moments of joy/peace/rest in the midst of terrifying fear or a horrific life event. How can that be? God's Grace is real. But you must recognize it, and take hold of it, pray for it, and give it to others, when you are sure you have no resources left to share: a smile, a kind word, praying for and with others. It can be draining; the thought of giving to others when you are spent is a crazy one. That's how you know God's Grace is sufficient.

You can't imagine how many times, while working, talking to a friend, family members, or my own kids I was having the same silent conversation with God, albeit, a one-sided discussion: "If You don't hurry up and save me, everyone is going to find out how crazy I really am. And you know that's my worst fear, Lord." Then I would realize that the person in front of me was expecting some type of response/acknowledgement. I'd pop back in to my cloaking stance, make the necessary gestures, movements, whatever, so that I could continue my exhausting/internal conversation with God. "God, You have a sense of humor but I'm not laughing anymore". "The truth is, I know better. I know that You exist. I know that You love me. I know that You created me for a special reason. But my faith is failing me. Why do I feel this way?" Another interruption would inevitably come my way. "Lord –

- I'm Scared that You think there's more to me, than I feel I can bear.

- I'm Scared that I will stumble and fall while my children are watching, my friends, neighbors and colleagues. I want to be selective of whom I show my crazy to.

- I'm Scared that I will live the rest of my days in physical pain, which is too much to comprehend. I want to get to heaven, but I cannot bare the pain you have allowed to flood my life much longer. Let me not shortcut the time here on earth you planned for me, please!

- Don't forget others (my sister Lord) who are waiting for a catastrophe to befall me and my family; and I don't understand why. They know that I am a believer. I am very verbal about who You are to me. Don't let me be embarrassed or put to shame. Where's the praise to You in that?

- Fear and his buddy trepidation are at my door, Lord. My house lights are turned off, and no one is home but me. I refuse to answer the door. But they won't leave. They keep ringing my doorbell. They are stalking me….

I Know You Are Here

Lord – I know you are here

I see your handiwork in my life, your warmth on the birds' songs

In my children's smiles

Lord – I know you hear

Why do you hide so gently from me?

Why do you not come to me?

I know you're here

I know you're here

I know you're here

I AM

Is here

Always been by my side

From the beginning to now

And will be there to welcome me home

Gentleness is your path through pain

All of My ways are not known to man

But what I share with you will suffice for your journey today

Walk and I will do the same with you

Run and I promise to be there before you arrive

Faith my Child, Have Faith

No Matter What You Face In Life

I Promise

You Will Never Face It Alone

Michelle Sommerset-Brown

CHAPTER TWENTY-SEVEN
You Gotta Try

I Gotta Try

Written By Michael MacDonald and Kenny Loggins

Performed By Michael McDonald

What Do You Do When You Don't Know What To Do?

Hold on.

Don't let go during your in-between. No matter what you see or hear. No matter if you feel all alone and unable to relate to the world and those around you.

Face Facts- Has God ever lied to you? Has He ever fallen short if His Word.

Fact: Something that actually exists➜ reality➜ truth: Fear and Faith cannot co-exist. It's an oxymoron.   If something is detrimental, one should remove himself or herself from it. But if something builds you up/secures/restores your position (spiritual maturity) in life, you should run toward it to fervently grab hold of your life line.

Why fear even after God has stated "So do not fear, for I am with you. Do not be dismayed for I am your God. I will help you and strengthen you with my righteous right hand."? Jeremiah 41:10, NIV

Think about it. You have been at the breaking point before. What's the difference now?

Your perception of how big your mountain is?

God is an expert mountain climber.

Sometimes not doing anything, is the perfect thing to do. Can you embrace the belief that the fastest way to get where you need to go, divinely, is by not taking one damn step, not one?

But instead, practice the art of releasing; of being, standing in the presence of God, and listening for his direction.

"If any of you lacks wisdom, he should ask God, who gives generously to all without finding fault, and it will be given to him. But when he asks, he must believe and not doubt, because he who doubts is like a wave of the sea, blown and tossed by the wind. That man should not think he will receive anything from the Lord; he is a double-minded man, unstable in all he does." James 1 vs. 3-6, NIV

Now the art of anything is just that. It's a way of being, it's fluid, but it always has a foundation on which to build. My foundation is God's Word – whether it is reflected in His Book of Life, the Bible, music and lyrics, a smile from a stranger, a prayer with a friend. God's essence, love, support, patience, protection, guidance can come from multiple sources. And His Truth is always clear, but not always heard. You have to be still and truly listen to hear Him.

You have to choose, even fight each day to listen/stand still, but most of all to accept the Truth. The truth that God/Jesus/Holy Spirit, one entity in three parts, is real and His promises are true.

Man typically believes the negative aspects of life. It's our nature. So you must fight each day to believe that Hope is possible and that Joy is around the corner. You must fight to be open to the wonders of life, yes, in the midst of what we may consider horrific life events. And at the end of many days, you will feel defeated and unsuccessful, yes. But God will reward your choice to believe in Him, no matter what you see or hear, with daily Grace to mount up on eagle's wings, to overcome, to forgive, and to love.

But You Gotta Try - to have faith, even after it is weakened from fatigue. That's when Grace does its best work…..

Go To Your Grave Fighting The Good Fight Of Faith!

CHAPTER TWENTY-EIGHT
Unwritten

Written By Brisebois, Danielle Bedingfield, Natasha Rodrigues,

Performed By Natasha Bedingfield

Three more days now, until my third and God willing, last ankle surgery. I'm in pretty severe pain as I write this chapter. It's emanating up my entire right hip. I know that my walk is imbalanced to counter the constant pain experienced in my ankle. Months and months of imbalanced walk-ing are starting to cause pain elsewhere in my body. I absolutely have to stay home and off this leg for two months at a minimum, as a result of a successful surgery. The memory of my post-operative pain is so vivid that I have to stop to write to try to get control of myself. But though I feel horrible at this moment, I have faith that my life is still unwritten.

The beauty of it all is HOPE. I still have lots of it left. Sure there have been dark days and many to come, but I still have hope.

I KNOW who walks with me.

I want a different life now. I want to be a published Author and a public speaker. I see myself signing books in multiple cities, with the biggest grin on my face. I see myself going anywhere I want to with no financial limitations. I see my husband and kids smiling at me with a nod of ap-proval. "Mom you made it." Yes, I told you guys that anything is possible and life can change for the better at any time, and for anyone, even me. I no longer want to work in Corporate America. I want Corporate Amer-ica to be my very best client.

Know this – There Are No Challenges, No Battles, No Obstacles that you cannot overcome. You will undoubtedly have many battle scars. A lifetime of scars can simultaneously generate a lifetime of smiles. All the bad in the world will never cancel out the Good.

Never, Ever, Ever Give Up.

Move forward, even if your trials seem to control your life. Move for-ward in God's Grace.

Don't Panic➔ Ask for God's Guidance➔

Follow His Instructions (Bible)➔Move Forward In Faith

Focus on taking the steps noted above, and allow God to guide and walk with you to the other side of your trial. Life will turn a corner. God promises you that fact, not me. But I sure can testify that His help is offered and rings true.

Walk through your Walk-A-"Bout"; with your buddy Jesus by your side. If you open yourself up to accept Jesus as your Savior today, you will never walk alone again. Life will be fuller for you.

CHAPTER TWENTY-NINE
Isn't It Ironic

Today is January 20, 2015. It's rather ironic to me that I was inspired to write all of the preceding chapters, not knowing that I would have to turn around so quickly to use them on myself, again. I got laid off today. It was not performance related. This month has been my highest revenue month. I made a sales call over the phone this morning. I closed the deal. Then not two hours later I got that call. I was told that I did not need to go on my scheduled client luncheon. But I replied that I had to go, because my partner was counting on me to close that deal. And I did. I smiled through the entire lunch as if nothing was wrong; as if my life had not been turned upside down, yet once again.

The company has been spiraling out of control for the last nine months, since our top executives got fired for reckless spending and mismanagement. It was only a matter of time for me to be impacted.

I know that this is premature - But I have faith that I will be able to say in short timing "Thank you CertusBank for laying me off". Why - Because it gave me motivation to finish the last two chapters of this book, and seriously start researching as of today the best way to get it published. I know that my book is a best seller because it is about the worst year of my life. I know that there will be so many people who will relate to what I have to say, and will buy it if only to feel like they can make it also; in spite of living through so many difficult moments. I went so far today as to write and recommend that Good Morning America start a one-year series, hosted by my favorite person "Robin" of course. The series could be, titled "Who Knew -- A Whole New You"! I never heard from them.

That's okay, God got back to me when I sought His face for guidance!

Don't Panic➜ Ask for God's Guidance➜

Follow His Instructions (Bible)➜Move Forward In Faith

Life Fundamentals

- Set Your Feet (Don't Let A Perceived Disaster Move You. Breathe, Ask for God's Guidance, Listen to The Instruction He Provides, Move Forward in Faith)

- Follow Through With Your Bat (Seek Godly Guidance and Follow His Instructions, Move Forward in Faith)

- Keep Your Eye On The Ball (Keep Your Eye on Jesus – No Matter What, Move Forward in Faith)

- You've Got A Full Count On You (2 strikes and three balls)– Now Protect Home Plate (Feed Your Spiritual Man – Daly, Don't Allow Satan To Steal It From You, Move Forward In Faith)

Thank you CertusBank for laying me off and pushing me to a "Whole New Michelle." I want everyone to know that it is not too late to have a new, successful, abundant and happy career. But most of all I want my kids to be proud of their mother.

It hasn't yet been a full weak since I got my pink slip. Some days have been better than others. But now I have more time to finish this book. My family and I went to our church today at First Baptist of Atlanta. Many of you may know our Pastor, Charles Stanley. I can't stop praising God for His perfect timing in having Pastor speak to my heart today. I'd like to share with you what I learned. I give all of the credit for the rest of this paragraph to God Almighty and Pastor Stanley for being obedient in delivering his message on, "Godly Guidance". It went something like this:

When you have to make a difficult decision, what do you do and who do you talk to? Read Psalm 32, vs. 7-11.

God promises to: instruct, teach and guide us through any and all of our life events, no matter how large or small they are; how seemingly important or unimportant to us. We are important to Him, with each breath that we take. God will guide your steps today and every day. As a Christian, you have the assurance of the Holy Spirit who works on your behalf through the will of God. The Spirit of God is the Counselor of all Counselors. The Counselor (Holy Spirit) will take time to listen to you; how you feel and your pain. The Counselor is always accountable to you, for what He guides you to do.

Please pay attention to what I am trying to tell you. If you listen to the wrong voice, it will cost you. God will never miss-lead you, but man in his human condition even in true friendship can lead you down a frightful path; that is, if his guidance is through the eyes of his flesh. Whomever you find yourself listening to, make sure that you lay down their advice next to the teachings of the Lord.

Are you at Ground Zero? Perfect – That may be the path necessary for God to get your attention and open your mind to the gifts, talents and skills you possess, which are untouched by anyone in this world.

CHAPTER THIRTY
You're Kidding, Right?

Do Everything

Written And Performed By Steven Curtis Chapman

You are not going to believe this.

What I am about to share with you was so shocking to me not only from a physical and mental state, but also from a spiritual perspective, that I literally felt like I was a walking zombie in the aftermath. The Big "BC", yes cancer came knocking on my door - breast cancer, that is. How in the hell did it find me? To my knowledge, no one in my family ever had this disease. How much can one person bare? Damn, Damn, Damnit!!!

Ductal Carcinoma in Situ is what it is called, Stage Zero, Grade III. We found it with my annual mammogram.

Let's review a couple of impactful events in my life:

1. Dad died.

2. Mom, off the chain.

3. Sister has always been off the chain, mean and hateful.

4. Aunt was just down right wrong at the wake (apologized, so I'll let that one go).

5. Lost my job in January – Got a severance package though – Wait for it!

6. Started a new job in May.

7. Found breast cancer the 1st of August.

8. Lost two breasts in September.

9. Oh – Had to take an unpaid medical leave, but required to pay the short-term disability that the company would not let me draw on.

10. Reconstruction surgery on my birthday, December 31, 2015, the last day of the year to avoid unnecessary medical bills for another surgery (which I could not afford) in a New Year.

Okay – Now God how am I supposed to make it through this one? Can you understand why I almost hit the floor in my office the day I was formally denied short-term disability? You're kidding me, right?

What's ironic about all of this is that the week before my surgery I had to volunteer, "Team Project", on a Habitat for Humanity Build Project. And two weeks before that our company intranet featured an article about helping starving individuals in our respective communities. I'll never forget the illustration of a red and white table cloth, a plate, fork and knife. I was so angry; my family would soon be the hungry ones needing a handout. I appealed to management to no avail. They had to see the illustration and irony as well.

In the midst of my knees bending in a position to hit the floor and slide under my desk, I heard a calm voice say to me, "Why do you think I laid you off in January?" The severance pay remaining will carry you through. God's voice prevented me from crying out to Him in agony to a cry of Praise – albeit in an instant. So here I am three weeks post a bi-lateral mastectomy – both sides of my back in stitches to help reconstruct my breasts – telling you a story of praise. My surgeon took three lymph nodes out – cancer free. No chemo and no radiation!

Yes, unexpected bills have cropped up, but I have not missed a bill yet and I have no credit card debt either. My prayer was that just as the story in the Bible tells us about how a loaf of bread and several fish fed thousands, that the money God gave me back in January would be sufficient to provide for my family and allow me a period of rest to heal. God came through for me as He always does. I hold Him in such reverence that I dare not ask, "Why Me". Why not? No matter what happens, He has proven to be true and faithful.

Another lesson in how to keep my faith alive!

CHAPTER THIRTY-ONE
My Book Of Woe….Whoa!

Look At Me Now

Beautiful Day

Written By Bruce Allen Miller, Kenny Flav

Performed By Jamie Grace

Look at me now.

I made it through such an awful period in my life.

I Finally Caught Myself Laughing

What started as my Book of Woe has turned in to

My Book of WHOA……

Now is my time and possibly yours, if you feel compelled to read this book, to "Breakout" and away from feelings of despair:

- To truly fight each day to _free your mind_ and heart to the possibilities of positive change in your daily life,

- To _open you up to the possibilities_ of a joyful life that can be lived in the midst of tragic life events.

- To embrace the knowledge that <u>*you will need tools to help you*</u> enjoy a successful life lived under God's Grace and Guidance.

I am placing all of my life chips on this one statement. It is never too late to change directions. To:

- Turn to Jesus, Your Savior who is waiting for you to ask for His help and mercy.

- Take up a new career and be successful at it. If you are reading this book one day, you'll know that I made it as a published author!

- Find your spiritually chosen path, which helps you achieve your dreams.

- Try a new way of thinking: Wake up with positive thoughts and expectations. Your life may depend on that one consistent behavior one day. Remember that if you want to wake up with positive thoughts and expectations, you have to go to sleep *making a conscious decision to water the flowers that you need to harvest each day.*

- Challenge yourself in ways that you never dared before. Take on more risks. My sons taught me that one. You're bound to find a sense of accomplishment and even joy in seeing yourself grow with and in Christ.

Above All, if you take this journey with me and you want to get out alive and victoriously, you must consider this:

God/Christ Jesus/Holy Spirit Alone Is The Only True "Go-To-Guy" He'll Never Drop Your Ball.

You don't have to be a Believer in Jesus Christ as your personal Savior. But mark my words, "You'll come to this realization one day." I'm counting on it.

Only You Lord – Let them See You In Me